THE ANSWER, IS IN YOU

REQUESTS FOR ANSWERS

from
Yogi Sally Ann Slight

(Pike)

ALL RIGHTS RESERVED.
NO PART OF THIS PUBLICATION MAY BE REPRODUCED,
STORED IN A RETRIEVAL SYSTEM, OR TRANSMITTED IN ANY FORM
OR BY ANY MEANS, ELECTRONIC, MECHANICAL,
PHOTOCOPYING OR OTHERWISE
WITHOUT THE PRIOR PERMISSION OF THE COPYRIGHT OWNER.

© COPYRIGHT 2020
SAS PUBLISHING.
DARTMOUTH, DEVON,
UNITED KINGDOM
Tel: 01803 363855

ALL RIGHTS RESERVED
PRINTED IN THE UNITED KINGDOM

ISBN 978-1910123-607
2nd Edition

For my sons George & Harry Slight

With the greatest of thanks to all the lovely people on
Facebook who shared their problems with me,
so that I could answer them.

You can also ask me a question on Facebook page,
"Sally Ann Slight"
and you will get an answer.

You have purchased this book (Thank you),
and so you can ask me a question that requires an answer.
I will reply, I look forward to it.

To now know that you can change your mind, is a great knowledge to learn, and it gives you the choice to remain in the emotion you find yourself in, or know there is another way, and make the correct decision to have a better day.

The problems you are in today are due to the thinking you had in the past. So to change your life, and to create a new pattern of life, is to change your thinking now, to experience a better life in the future.

The words of the solutions in this book, are of a different thinking. A thinking that brings you good results and creates a better life pattern to follow.

For only YOU can change your own mind.

I am so thankful to be an inspiration in your better life experiences.
Peace be with you as you read.
Sit, be still and smile...
Feel good in that smile and your journey begins....again.

.

.

.

.

.

.

.

THE MAP OF ASCENSION

...so you know where you are
...how far you have come
...how far you may still have to go

...and you can choose which direction to head in!

Peace
Serenity
Joy
Respect
Love
Understanding
Forgiveness
Optimism
Trust
Courage
pride/indifference
anger/hate
desire/craving
fear/anxiety
grief/regret
apathy/despair
guilt/blame
shame/humiliation

Where are you now?
Where do you want to be?

You used to jump because you were happy.

Then you started to jump to make yourself happy.

Your best jumps were when you were happy.
Your safe jumps were when you were happy.
You can only jump when you are happy.

You cannot jump to make yourself happy.
You have to be happy to jump.

SMILE...

BE THANKFUL...

BREATHE....

breathe in long and slow to the count of 3....
breathe out long and slow to the count of 5......

You will feel the joy expand within you...
because you know it is the happiness that creates the best jump.

You create happiness by your breathing in the happiness and thankfulness.

3 in...
5 out...
Long and slow....

BREATHING clears your mind to accept the happiness....

OK?

.

.

.

Eddie Kidd (stunt rider) said.....OK!

HOW TO GET OUT OF YOUR OWN QUESTIONING LEVEL?

You have asked your question, now...

Sit

Be still

Smile

Think...
"Thank you,
Thank you,
Thank you."

You may feel that Smile now deep in your tummy,
It feels Good and you keep Smiling.

Breathe deeply and slowly

*

Keep Smiling

Keep feeling Good

*

Breathe deeply and slowly

Keep Smiling

Smile

UNIVERSAL LAW

7 Keys that Affect Reality and Good Health.

Everything in the Universe obeys the same Laws.
These natural laws govern creation and existence.

They are consistent and they are everywhere,
and each one holds an important key to creating balance
and harmony within yourself and your life's experiences.

When you understand these 7 laws
and apply them to your daily living,
you learn to control yourself,
your environment and everything in it.

To begin, it is important to state that
the first 3 of the Universal Laws of the Universe are...
<u>IMMUTABLE</u>
meaning they cannot be changed.
Unchanging over time.

And the last 4 are...
<u>MUTABLE</u>
liable to change, changeable.

Each of these Laws exist in nature and work directly with our
Mental, Emotional, Spiritual and *Physical* states.

By understanding and implementing these laws,
you have the wisdom to take charge of your life,
influence your environment
and direct your personal journey.

Temperamental
=
*Temper a*ffects your *mental* health...

.

.

.

IT IS NOT THE VESSEL THAT IS TO BLAME,
BUT THE CAPTAIN OF THE SHIP.
AND SOMETIMES HOWEVER MUCH THE CAPTAIN WANTS TO GET IT RIGHT,
SOMETHING GOES WRONG.
SO WE LEARN FROM OUR MISTAKES.

Just as in good health, the will, (the Captain of your body) makes a decision and the body tries to complete its command.......
but the body knows exactly what it is meant to do,
and unless the two commands are exactly alike,
the outcome will be something getting hurt.

And in health, it will always be the body getting sick or staying in good health,
just because the will decides on a new plan.

Your Mind is a wonderful piece of equipment, used correctly.
Your body is a wonderful piece of equipment when you let it get on with its purpose.....
and that is to keep your Spirit safe and on this planet for as long as possible....
A bit like a space suit for a man on the moon!

The body is already programmed for perfection and comes fitted with all the latest equipment to keep the Spirit, encapsulated and functioning correctly for many, many years of pleasure on this planet.

.....but, BUT.....when you start to focus on the body,
rather than the purpose you signed up to accomplish on this planet,
that is when you are out of alignment with Body and Mind.

As you are only focusing on the body, so the Mind loses focus on your assignment,
on your mission here!

............................So, you say, "Yes, but I have this disease, and I need to look after my body and so I have asked some people in white coats, that are called Doctors, to also look at this body that is not functioning correctly."

............and we say,"Because over time, over loads of time, you have been focusing on your body all the time, you have been criticizing it and making it feel unloved, so it has broken down....

It is equipped with all the latest technology and was in tip top condition, yet you decided that it didn't look like the other people, that you loved, and so you let yourself get down.
And you tried to recreate its cells and expand them, shrink them, remove them, add to them, rearrange them and generally not want what you have......
And it is all that you have!

It is all you were given to keep you on this planet and to do the job you were assigned to do.
Have you forgotten what you were assigned to do???
Well, have you?

We thought so!"

So, now we have to bring your space suit back to some sort of semblance of self and update your Mind to understand that your suit is perfect.

It is a mass of cells that are programmed to keep Spirit on this planet for a very long time.
And we appear to have to keep repeating this information because your Mind sorta, kinda wanders off, like a child following a butterfly flitting across a meadow of wild flowers.....
And we, the Mother Ship have keep hailing you back to path!
To get you to try to remember what it was that you were assigned to do on this planet.

But sitting still and allowing us to link in with you is tiresome isn't it....
(we call it Mediation, you however are focusing more on Medication!).

Now, we have your attention we can now say,
without any error on our part,
that YOU ARE HEALTHY NOW.........

And you just have to let the spacesuit/body get on with everything it is programmed to do.....

Have Faith in your suit/body, and KNOW THAT YOU ARE WELL, NOW!.........

Any twinges, fluttering, vomiting or pains, and breakages are you completely out of alignment with your true self....
And your true self is Energy,
that flows absolutely perfectly and keeps you in perfect health.

You watch so many 'other' programs that worry you about health.
That keeps people employed,
for they too have forgotten how wonderfully healthy they all are too,
and they live in fear of death,
that they actually create by their fear and lack of understanding of Faith in Self...

So, it will take some time to actually Believe in yourself and how fantastic you really are....
and getting it slightly wrong.

But now can you understand (if you want to) that your sickness is your own Belief in it...?

Your breakage can mend,
and so too can the dark thoughts you like to rely on,
that bring you fear of having to leave this planet.

Yet, if you would just rely on your body/suit.
That it is just how you wanted it, and needed it to be to survive in the environment that you have chosen to habitat.

You knew you had to learn the best foods to eat and not eat,
yet you still make yourself sick by consuming everything!....everything!

Sit, be still and listen to what you need right now.....

and you will probably find that you do not actually need anything.

And your wonderful body is programmed to switch on the hunger, thirst and removal modes correctly at the exact moment that you need them......
Peace be with you

The 1st Law is the
LAW of MENTALISM

This Law states that all is Mind, the Universe is mental.

Everything we see and experience in our physical world
originates from the invisible mental realm.

This governs all outward manifestations in our material world.

Everything that is apparent to our physical senses is in actuality Spirit,
and that Spirit is One Universal Consciousness or Mind.

What appears to be separate is actually connected,
everything you think and therefore do,
is an interaction of thought with thought.

Through the power of your mind, you influence your existence.

Your thought also has an effect on an energetic level,
your mind is a part of the one Universal Mind
and your reality is a manifestation of your mind.

All of the world, and or Universe
is a manifestation existing in the Mind of the All,
or more simply stated,
the underlying reality of the Universe is Mind.

This Law allows the person to use the other Laws to effect change.

This Law is Immutable.

THERE WAS A REQUEST FOR HEALING FOR A FRIEND....

MY REPLY... you can tell him......
his belief in sickness creates more of it......!

All those little thoughts have grown into a larger more profound one now, that he has also shared with others to prove his own diagnosis.

He is perfect.
He has to over come his belief in dis-ease = not at ease with self.

And he will save himself.....
so he can stay longer for his family.

Time to slow down and rest in the knowledge that his health will be the health of his world too.

To turn the effect around.....
to heal the world is to heal oneself,
by thoughts of perfection and turn away from the path of sickness.

For it is only a thought, and one that does not serve him, or his family, or his world at this time.

I do hope you will pass this message onto him....
and I hope he understands that HE IS THE CENTER OF HIS OWN IMAGINATION THAT CREATES HIS LIFE EXPERIENCE.

Peace be with you all
Yogi Sally Ann Slight

The 2nd Law is the
LAW of CORRESPONDENCE

This embodies the truth that there is
Harmony, Agreement and Correspondence
between the
Spiritual, Mental and Physical realms.

As above, so below.
As below, so above.
As within, so without.
As without, so within.

There is no separation because everything within the Universe
resides in the One Universal Mind.

The same pattern is expressed on all planes of existence
from the smallest electron to the largest planet and vice versa.

Therefore, there is always correspondence
between the Laws and the various planes of existence.

The Energetic and Spiritual plane
directly corresponds with the Physical plane,
and the Energy you project with your Physical body,
via your Thoughts, Beliefs and Emotions,
directly correspond with the Spiritual realm.

This law enables a person to reason intelligently
from the known to the unknown,
meaning you can use your individual mind
to reach into the other areas of the Universal Mind,
to find solutions to any, or all, perceived difficulties.

This Law is Immutable.

A religion can state that you are perfect,
your thoughts about your imperfection create more of all that you think is imperfect...
because you believe in imperfection.....!

Imperfection and dis-ease are your thought demons (they are your negative thoughts that keep you in your current situation).

When you start to love yourself again and forgive the past completely.....
(there are ways to do that correctly),
your body returns to the perfection it always has been..............
The cells are perfect, (they used to be)
yet they listen to your thoughts about all you think you are,
all that you believe in,
and have been told that you are,
and so they do as they are told.....

You are the Captain of your body ship and your cells are the crew,
they obey your thoughts and words......
So it is up to you, Captain, to change your thoughts and words about yourself.

Every time you tell people about your dis-ease, you make that belief stronger.
Once you understand you can change your reply to others without harming yourself more,
you stop and think first before you speak....
And in so doing, you change the way the cells react to your thoughts and beliefs, because YOU are actually believing in yourself and your power over your own beliefs in dis-ease.

Dis-ease = not at ease with yourself.

Start gently and easily with....

"I am returning to perfection.
I know this will take some time to turn this ship around,
but I feel I am back on course again now and I really like the idea of returning to perfection....

I am really starting to love myself again.
I look at myself and think kinder thoughts about myself.

I speak kind words about myself and about others.
I like to see the good in my life now.....
I like to be thankful for all the good in my life now,
and I am thankful that I have been given the chance to turn my life around....
I know it is my choice now,
and I have decided to not let myself down and keep good thoughts and kinder words in my life,
about myself, and about others."

You will carry on with all your Doctors requests, and yet you have this thought in the back of your mind now, that you are returning to perfection.
And this higher will of yours will keep you on course.
You will feel better quicker and your stats will astound your Doctors.

Goodness keeps you on course,
you feel good in goodness.
When you feel bad, you have gone off course, and you have to accept that you have to change a whole load of thoughts that you used to think about the world....(that got you into this mess).

Take it easy, one step at a time,
one day at a time,
being kinder to yourself and others......

Get yourself a guide who can keep you on course and you will reach your perfect destination of Good Health.

Peace be with you
Yogi Sally Ann Slight
.
.
.
.

.
Live your life, love her anyway, smile and be pleasant anyway......
Only say kind words, and walk away if she does not.
Find something you like to do because this is all about you.
....just as she has made it her choice to upset you at this time....that is her choice,
and you also have your own choices.

Stay being the fantastic you that you are,
love everyone and enjoy the day.

Everything in the past has now been forgotten (because you choose that too).
The next moment is always yours to choose what great thing you would like to do or say now.

You are lovely, stay that way up on your high level of love.
She will learn by watching you, not by you telling her anything.

OK....Peace be with you and enjoy every moment of your lovely day
Yogi Sally Ann Slight

.
.
.
.
.

Memories are surfacing through your dreams.
Your low level of emotion at this time of year is bringing you memories of the same level of emotion.

Find something that makes you happy, keep doing that, and your dreams and memories will also be good.
You create more good times by being in a happy and good emotional state.

And that is always your choice.

Peace be with you
.
.
.
.

Does it feel good?

Alignment with your inner source feels good, so if it does not feel good, you are not aligned with your best life experience are you.

Do what feels good.

Peace be with you

The 3rd Law is the
LAW of VIBRATION

The Law of Vibration states that nothing rests,
everything moves,
everything vibrates.

The whole Universe is vibration,
everything we experience through our Physical senses
is in fact vibration.

The difference between the different manifestations of
Mind, Matter and Energy
largely results from varying states of vibration.

For example...
Sound is Light at a lower vibration
&
Light is Sound at a high oscillation.

Thoughts and emotions are also vibrations
and the Law of Attraction itself has it's foundation in this Law.

Understanding vibration and frequency,
and learning to control mental vibrations at will,
gives a person the unique power to have authority over their reality.

This Law is Immutable.

Smile sweetly and ask him if he had a good holiday....
Make him a cup of tea....
Be the bigger person.

Love your job....
the people can be walked away from, when you go home.

You have shut the door and you smile and say,
"Phew, that was an interesting day, thankfully I am going home now to my loved ones and enjoy their company."

.....and enjoy the rest of your day.

Peace be with you

.

.

.

.

.

Yes, when you understand.....fear is living in the future mind my dear.

Your past fear created this unease, that you are experiencing NOW...
Your beliefs in the future fear keep you in fear....
Your beliefs in bad rather than good, keeps you in fear.

So, in this moment NOW, do you have all you need?

Moment to moment give thanks for all the good there is in your life NOW.
When you speak kindly about yourself, and others, you are at ease.
When you think kindly about yourself, and others, you are at ease.

So smile,
Be at ease.
Be kind.
Speak good words.

You are creating your better future NOW!

Peace be with you

.

The 4th Law is the
LAW of POLARITY

This is the first of the 'Mutable Laws' and it states,
everything is dual,
everything has poles,
everything has its pairs of opposites.

Like and unlike are the same,
opposites are identical in nature but different in degree.

Extremes meet.
All Truths are but half truths.
All paradox's may be reconciled.
(A paradox is a statement that may seem contradictory
but can be true, or at least make sense...
Save money, by spending it.
If I know one thing, it's that I know nothing...etc)

In everything there are 2 poles or opposite aspects.
Opposites are actually the same thing,
they vary only in degree.
They are in fact identical in nature,
they are the 2 extreme sides of the very same thing.

Love & hate,
Black & White,
Hot & Cold,
Peace & war,
Light & darkness
and even
Energy & Matter.

Just as you have the ability to transform
your Thoughts and Emotions from hate to Love,
you can equally transform your Energy into Matter.

continued...

Smile,
Congratulations...
You felt your own good!
Bouncing off of them and back at you!!

When you approach another your vibe gets to them before you do...
If they are not accepting that vibe, it bounces off of them and back at you!
And that is why we get into so much trouble girls!
We think it's them that feels good, it is actually yourself, open and receptive to loving everyone....

So, when you feel that again, is it your equal?
or is it them returning your love?

So it is the 2nd step that is the one where you know if it is love, and the 3rd...etc.

Put God first, then watch behaviour, kindness in words and deeds to find the real person you instantly fell in love with...

It only took me 55years to figure this out.

Peace is easier than love, to welcome another.

Peace be with you too

Smile...
Love yourself more
Be thankful that you are wonderfully made...
Not mad!!!

Peace be with you

LAW of POLARITY cont.

We can change our perception of the degree of an opposite,
by recognizing that it has that degree.

In other words,
you can choose that any perceived difficulty you currently have in your life,
is but only one degree of something else,
something that actually has the opposite of that.

There are different expressions of the same thing,
and because you already have one of them,
you only need to focus and change your energy
to be fixated on another degree of that.

It is not an obstacle that needs to be overcome,
rather it is something you already have
that you only need to choose which degree to focus on.

"The opposite of any perceived difficulty
already exists as a part of it.
In every perceived failure lies success.
It is only a matter of varying degree."

This Law is mutable.

Smile....
the receptors in your face kick start all the good stuff inside....

So even if you don't find anything to be happy about,
the work you need to do is SMILE.....
Just like you go to the gym to build muscles,
you build happiness with smiling.

Yes, it really is that easy.
The better you feel in your deep smile,
the better the thoughts that come to mind.
You are rising upwards to the good thought stuff,
the peaceful words and loving kindness, wisdom and choice.

Its all good stuff when you SMILE....

Peace be with you

.

.

.

.

.

Sweetheart, every day is a new day to fall in love with the special one you have
.....love everything that is in your life.

Make those special dates and things that made you love him in the first place.....
He changes every day too.

So to keep love, you have to give love.
Be thankful you have someone who loves you.
Be thankful for all the good in your life, and you feel good about yourself and the special other in your life.

Do you still love yourself?
....then loving everyone else is easy.

Be so thankful you are loved.
Be thankful you are alive today, to live in love again.

Peace be with you child.
.

You are taught to be unhappy,
to complain, to not be thankful,
...to not grow in goodness and kindness.

You have to work at being kind in a world where you don't hear much about kindness and peace, love and happiness.

You have to make your own happiness and do what makes you feel good and not listen to bad news, sad stories and gossip.

It is now your choice...

Now you know....oh dear, now you know!

Smile, keep smiling and feel good in that smile....
be thankful for all the good in your life
and you will get good thoughts that create your better life.

It really is up to you to know what makes you happy,
because only you knows what makes you happy.

It is not the same for everyone....
your happiness is as different to another's.
Yet, it is always basically the same.

So, what makes you happy?
....do that, and then more things that make you happy.

Your happiness grows and your mental health becomes clear and healthy....
happiness is good health.

and that really is the Truth.

Peace be with you on your new Journey to good health.
.
.
.
.
.
.

Yes, you manifested what you wanted my dear, then he decided to unlike it because he remembered.
He took control of his life again.
He felt your thought for him, he responded, and then he remembered.

Yes, you can manifest people, but wouldn't you rather they contacted you because they want to, rather than from a 'thought order' from you.

Watch Alice in Wonderland and even though, both the White and Red Queens manifest, one does it by love the other does it by fear.

It is always your own choice who you love, let them have their choice too, or you will have endless heartache in this life.

Peace be with you child.
.
.
.

.
You are just experiencing all those bad thoughts and words from the past...
They have finally caught up with you.

So, now you start speaking kind words about yourself,

Kind words about others
And
Kind words about the world.

You are then creating your better tomorrows and good future.
It's up to you.
You have proof now that horridness creates more of the same.
Create more good times in the future by speaking kind words about yourself,
About others, and about the world and everything in it.

Only you can turn this ship around Captain!

Enjoy the journey, set sail and keep your sea calm.

Peace be with you.
.
.

The 5th Law is the
LAW of RHYTHM

This Law states that everything flows, out and in.
Everything has its tides, all things rise and fall.

The pendulum swing manifests in everything,
the measure of the swing to the right
is the measure of the swing to the left.

Rhythm compensates.

We can easily see this Law in Action
with the tides of the ocean,
in business trends and cycles,
life and death,
creation and destruction,
and even how our Thoughts can move
from Positive to negative and back again.

Nothing stops, it is always changing.

When a person understands this Law they can polarize
to the degree of the swing that they desire on the pendulum,
to keep from being swung back to the other extreme.

To do this you must become aware of the subtle swing back
in a movement and not allow discouragement or fear to set in.

Keep your thoughts focused on your outcome,
as in the example given in the Law of Polarity...
and remain consistent in your endeavours,
no matter how far back this transitory Law pulls you.

And most reassuring is, that this Law states that
you must be pulled back to the other side in doing so.

This Law is mutable.

Yes, you are a slave to the Rhythm!!
....and now you know that.
You can choose the emotional level you wish to experience,
and you can choose to stay there.

With practice of course!
.
.

.
Oh dear he was not brought up in a time when they believed much in positive thought, was he!

...........the past is gone.

.....have a great day and a fantastic tomorrow.

Peace be with you too.
.
.
.

.
Forgiveness means, nothing happened in the past....
it did not happen.!

....so there is nothing to forgive is there!.....

.....and when you know this and feel this.....
then you are privileged to know you are forgiven,
and you find it easier to forgive others......

because it didn't happen....did it!

Peace be with you.
.
.

.
A simple sorry will suffice....
and if they don't accept that, then that is their choice.

You carry on in your own happiness.

Peace be with you child.
.

The 6th Law is the
LAW of CAUSE & EFFECT

Every Cause has its Effect.
Every Effect has it's Cause.

Everything happens according to the Law.

Chance is but a name for, 'Law Not Recognized'.

There are many planes of Causation,
but nothing escapes the Law.

Every Effect that is seen in the outside physical world,
has a very specific Cause,
which has it's origin in the inner Mental world.

The Conscious Creator makes the conscious choice
to rise above any circumstance
they no longer wish to experience.

They choose the degree or expression to focus upon,
they recognise the swing of the Rhythm,
and remain steadfast,
and they become the Cause
that creates the Effect they choose.

They know that the Law of Cause & Effect
begins on the Spiritual plane,
where everything is instantaneous.

Having this awareness,
gives the Conscious Creator,
the ability to rule their own plane.

This Law is mutable.

To be in a low emotion will not bring to you the answer you require from yourself.

Smile, and be thankful for all the goodness you have in your life at this time....(a roof over your head, clothes, food, good health etc.).

Go for a walk in the countryside if you can, start to feel better, and the answer will come to you when you start to feel better about yourself.

You have to put in the work to get the good answer,
and the work is always giving Thanks,
for the good you already have, so then you can have more.
See how easy it is!

You know what you really want,
and the only thing that is blocking your good answer to your life, is YOU,
and your low thoughts that keep you feeling sad.

Smile, be thankful, be happy, you will get good thoughts,
you will know what to do for your new life.

Peace be with you too.
.
.
.
.
.

Happiness is the opposite to sadness,
so to make Happiness, you have to know Happiness.

Be thankful for all the good in the world, and be kind to yourself in thought word and deed....

only YOU knows what makes YOU happy.....

Yes, you can be anything, and with everything you want to be there can be Effects that you may not want to experience.

Take every day in Love and Happiness, Kindness and Peace and you feel better sooner.

Peace be with you too.
.

The 7th Law is the
LAW of GENDER

Gender is in everything,
everything has it's masculine and feminine principles.
Gender manifests on all planes.

This Law is easier to explain
as we know that both male & females exist in both humans and animals.
But this masculine & feminine energy also exists in
plants, electrons, magnetic poles
and in the creative nature of all things on all planes.

Within every woman lies all the latent qualities of a man
and within every man those of a woman.
Nothing can come into being without the use of both of these energies.

The masculine contains a conquering assertive,
explorative and future driven energy.
Whereas, the feminine contains a receptive,
nourishing, protective and present energy.

These energies balance each other.

Gender is responsible for creation,
generation and regeneration.

By examining our own lives
and determining how balanced we are
with each of these energies,
we can adjust ourselves accordingly
to create our desires in a more effortless way,
when we balance the two.

This Law is mutable.

Sit, be still.....
see yourself in both jobs, going to work, coming home...
which one feels better?

....always go with the one that feels good.

Peace be with you.

.
.
.
.

Remember all the good things in your life and be thankful for them.

Smile and feel good in that smile.....
and KNOW in this moment now, "I am good."

....Peace be with you child.

.
.
.
.

Confidence is not being big headed,
it is the art of loving yourself and happy being around others, whatever happened in the past.

Confidence = confide = speak to your inner self and you will always hear...
"I love you."

.......and that really makes you feel good.

And smile in that feeling if goodness......

You are good,
You are loved,
You are fantastic.

Peace be with you child.

.
.
.
.

Teach her to write of all the good things in her life.
Her good memories.
Her good plans for the future.
If she will not listen to you telling her this, write her this letter and pop it under her door..

"To my darling child,
your happiness is in your own hands now, you are old enough to learn this.
You make you happy! You can do this for yourself, and I can share with you this secret, it is time for you to know this now.
Here it is.......
When you think of all the good you have in your life and you are thankful for it, you feel better.
When you remember all the good times from your past, and are thankful for them, you feel better.
When you start daydreaming and imagining how great your future will be, you feel better.

You have your room to write about all the good in your life,
all your memories and all your plans for the future.
Take your time.

I will buy you some more notepads, and pens, to write all the goodness that you have, you are, and you will be in them.
If you need any help remembering how wonderful and happy you were in the past, I will be sending you some more notes to remind you.
You are in control now, and I know you can reach your goal of Happiness, now I have given you the tools.
You know I love you, now its time for you to love you again.
I can wait, and you can speak to me when you are ready.

Peace be with you my darling child.
Love Mum XXXXXXX

..........and then you wait.
And send loving thoughts,
think only good thoughts and smile more,
because you KNOW everything is going to be alright now.

Peace be with you too.

Impulse = I'm pulse = I am pulse = I am the very thing that breathes you...

I know what you need...

Ask me.....(not me the writer, your inner you)

....OK!..........................

Peace be with you.
.
.
.
.
.

What sin?
It is forgotten, forgiven, it did not happen, it is gone.

Now, live a good life and peace be with you.

God is good.

Peace be with you.
.
.
.
.
.

Things you think,
Things you say,
Things you do....

Choose lovely things!

Peace be with you too.
.
.
.
.

You still haven't got the hang of forgiveness yet ???

Peace be with you
.

Smile,
I am already peaceful,
Thanks.

I'm just waiting for the rest of you to catch up!

Peace be with you too

.

.

.

Actually,
You are perfect!
You are just caught up in an illusion of sickness.

When you focus only on good health, goodness in the world and good in everyone.
Then you too have good health.

Focus at this time on clear blue skies and sunshine.
Breathing in that imagination
And
Breathing out all the horridness that you have kept in your belief over all these lifetimes.

It really is a good world, and so are you.

You are your thoughts my dear, and you are perfect when you begin to turn your thoughts around, and return to your perfection.

Your thoughts created what is in you, your beliefs have held onto those thoughts, you now know of your perfection... and you can head towards that goal.

Good health is a Superpower my dear, never sickness.

You can be a Victor and no longer a victim of your mind, and all that it creates.
Overcome sickness with good thoughts, kindness to others and peace be with you.

Have a lovely day.

.

Step by step in happiness and trust.
Brick by brick in building.

You believe in what you want to....
Just as I believe in what I want to.

You say its fake,
I believe it is real.
I believe that it is Truth.

I feel better knowing that it is real.

We have to believe don't we!!???

And sometimes we believe what we want to.
And as we believe, we can change things.

Peace be with you.

The illusion gains energy by focusing upon it...
So focus on rain or sunshine my dear.
That is also an illusion.

It's up to you.

Focus on what you want..
Always.

Peace be with you

My dear, by having a picture of something, creates more focus on that....
Whether you want it or not!

If you want PEACE,
show pictures of peace and words of peace.

Now you know.

There is rain, and even if it is a small amount, that can bring more.
Bringing happiness by this news creates more happiness and more rain, which is what we want.
Keep asking for what you want.
Do not mention what you do not want.

Show more pictures of what you want...

Peace be with you

You are forcing rather than allowing.
Just be still, allow and keep the goodness that you are.
It is all good.

You are healed, you are perfect, and so the path is created, you enjoy the journey.

Every moment be thankful.

Live in happiness of the moment.

Peace be with you

Forgive and keep on loving them.

It feels better that way.
Then it's up to them to change for the better.
It is a choice.

Smile
Focus on all the good things in life and be thankful for them.

It pushes all bad thoughts away.

Peace be with you child
.
.
.
.

R ealizing
I
C reate
H appiness

and then...

R emembering
I
C reate
H appiness

Thank you.
.
.
.
.

Smile,
Congratulations

It is also to remind you to remain in the present moment in thanks....

So thankful for all the good in my life.

Phew, that feels better.

Peace be with you too
.
.
.
.

It seemed right at the time.
It was my best choice at the time.
I knew no better for myself.
Thankfully, we grow in choices too.

Peace be with you

Pain is due to lack of love

Pain is due to your judgement upon another.

Pain is due to you being out of alignment with your inner spirit,
Who actually loves everyone.

Pain is due to your mind and your choice of thoughts.

Love is the spirit within.

Love never harms us,
Your thoughts about another harm yourself...
Yet you blame them!

Be responsible for your thoughts,
You have the choice.

Love keeps your friends.

Peace be with you

Remove the word 'NEVER'....

Phew, that feels better.
You will understand why later.

Peace be with you too

Smile,
You already know the answer!
So, now it is easier to change the mind.

What are you thankful for?
From the past and in the present moment...?

Just keep thinking about all the good stuff and
You push away all the lower thoughts
and create a habit of good thinking.

Easy really, now you know!

Peace be with you

.

.

.

Smile,
"Can you manage everything that you need to accomplish in this moment? "

Yes
or
No?

Yes....
Then you are good enough.

or
No...
You haven't understood the question!
Read it again.

And every moment asks you the same question

And so
you keep asking,
and you keep replying...

"In this moment, NOW............................ Yes!"

Phew, that feels better.

.

Depression is not real when you change your mind to a better feeling thought....it can be done.
You just have to want to change your mind.

And if you did not know that, well, now you do, and it is always your choice as to what thought you want to accept into your head.

If it feels bad, breathe in and say,
"I want a better feeling thought please."

and then breathe out and say,
"THANK YOU"

....and you will get a better feeling thought,
and then it becomes automatic after practice.

And your whole life changes,
because you are planting good words rather than horrid ones.
Your past bad words and thoughts have actually grown into the feelings you are experiencing now.

And only you know what you think and feel, and the proof is the experience you are living in now.

Take some time, and start thinking about all the things you love and that are good in your life now.
You are then starting your better tomorrows.
And that makes you disciplined in your own mind and you have a good life.
You can only prove this to yourself,
no one else can do it for you.

And if you keep chatting about all the horrid things you are going through,
Guess what,
you go through more of them!
Oh dear!

Now you know this, I hope you will find the good words and have a better life.

Peace be with you

Smile,
What's good now?
What was good then?

Think about that
And
You create your tomorrows

So what is there to worry about!!!?????

Smile
And choose only the good thoughts

Speak kind words

Peace be with you

Smile
Congratulations,
You always get an answer when you want one

Peace be with you child

Love people,
and then you might notice that they actually change around you

....it really is worth the effort.

Peace be with you

That is correct my dear,
yet by mentioning all that you do not want, is to increase that too.!

Write a post that mentions only what you want.

Peace be with you child

Oh, my dear, you are experiencing the Law of Rhythm...
Backwards and forwards, in the Law of Polarity and Mentalism.

You can choose to remain in all that is good, rather than keep swinging too and fro from one to the other.

It is all choice my dear.

Smile,
You are Love.
And you remind them that they are not so loving as you.

They will have some work to do to be more loving.
Some do not want to bother.

Peace be with you

REMEMBER!

you are just interacting
with a thought...

IS IT YOURS?

Love always works best in a relationship.

Thoughts, words, actions and feelings of love....

Anything else just isn't being in love is it...?

Peace be with you

Unconditional love.

A totally different feeling in love.

Peace be with you

Do we have to accept things we cannot change?

Surely if we cannot change them, we don't have to accept them either!

We accept only what we want to accept.
Focus on what you want and all the good in your life.
Be thankful for all the good in your life now.

That changes your vibe and more good happens.
Only you can do this for yourself ok!

Peace be with you

Love always works best in a relationship!

Thoughts of love.
Words of love.
Acts of love.
Feelings of love.

Find those feelings of love,
And stay in the now.
Thankful for all you have now,
In love.

Peace be with you child
.
.
.

Smile...
Feel good
Have good thoughts

Peace be with you child
.
.
.

Good...
Keep on caring,
Keep on loving them,
Keep smiling....

Your higher vibe affects them in ways you may never know.

Peace be with you child
.
.
.

Smile
Forgive...Forgive...Forgive

Know that behaviour is learnt from others,
who knew no better at the time too.

Forgive....Things get better when you forgive.
Peace be with you
.

To talk it out my dear!?
...it is already out, is it not?

You are experiencing your worries and fears already,
so why would you want to create more of the same?

Your words and thoughts create, my dear,
they created all that you now experience.

So, from this moment on, what are you thankful for?
What good is there in your life at this moment that you are thankful for now?
This moment now, what are you thankful for?

And now you create your better tomorrows.
Start feeling good and more good will come to you.

Yes, it really is that easy.
The proof is all that you now experience....!

You know you have been worried,
and so you experience your worry.
Only you know what thoughts you accept (yes, you accept them) and what judgements you have spoken.

So now accept better thoughts.
Speak kinder words,
and they create good feelings and good feelings keep you healthy, wealthy and wise my dear.

So, what are you thankful for in this moment now?
Enjoy the process of creating your good tomorrows by accepting the good thoughts of today.

Peace be with you

.
.
.

.
Money is not the root of all evil...
it is energy just like everything else !

.
.

Smile,
Congratulations,
Now you know you have to stay in your own mind.

Do what you want to do, and pull him up to your level my dear.

That's all anyone wants,
Is to be happy.

So be happy.
And you might find, he was only being down, because you were!!!

Peace be with you and your family

Keep trusting.
Keep loving.
Keep smiling.

That keeps you in a higher level of emotion where nothing harmful can be in your experience...
because it doesn't exist!

Remember, when you are with other people you are in their experience...
You can step out just as easily as you stepped in.

Be kind in your thoughts as you enter,
wipe your feet as you leave.

Peace be with you

Smile,
Good thoughts create good feelings my dear.

So, to be dumped, creates loads of bad thoughts.
Unless you know that you have a choice.

To accept the bad thoughts or....
Forgive yourself and go back to thinking and speaking goodness and kindness,
about everything and everyone.
To love again, your self and others.

The more you practice the easier it becomes, and then virtually automatic good thoughts are created everyday.

Have perfection as your goal.
And so you have something to aim for.

"I am perfect.".. Its taken many years but its all worth it.

And then sometimes....
I'm not perfect, and I have to remember that I am,
and so I choose a good thought again.

Peace be with you
.
.
.

.

I found I wanted to actually be like Jesus.
Then all the weird stuff started to happen.

Then ego kicked in and I carried on as if it was me.
Then God removed everything and I was happier than before.
Then God made me wait for everything He said I could have.

Then I had to ask for help.
Then I knew it was all part of the story.
Then I knew I could change the story.
Then.....

Its not over yet is it!!!!

It's about belief and knowledge and then just belief...

And then.....

I'm happy anyway, and isn't that all we are meant to be...
To be healthy.
It's fun though and I am thankful.

What's going to happen next?
Everything wonderful!!!

Peace be with you too
.
.
.
MY REPLY ON FORGIVENESS

Every thought that feels bad,
Can be exchanged for a good thought.

A good thought is one where you actually look for the good in the person...or situation.
It takes practice, but that is forgiveness.
Look at it, as a gift to yourself.
Your good health is created by good thoughts.

So give 4 good thoughts
To every bad thought.
Give4 good thoughts
4give

Turn a bad thought around.
Give 4 good thoughts to replace it.

You will thank yourself for it...
As it is only you who harms yourself with bad thoughts.

You live in good health in good thoughts.
You have more good thoughts about all sorts of things, when you practice more.

You will find some good in this person,
And the more you look,
The more you will see.
Peace be with you
.

Learning about the bad things people do to each other actually prepares
you for the experience!

Read more about, 'How to Love one another',
to enable a good relationship.

All that you watch,
And all that you read,
Are seeds you are planting,
Either flower or weed!

Thoughts of the past and future makes you anxious my dear,

Are you OK Now?
In this moment now, do you have everything you require?

Then that creates your mind of peace.

And when you believe that bad thought about someone....
You harm yourself.

Everyone has the ability to control and choose their thoughts,
when they are informed that they can !

Blimey, if you believe you harm another by your bad thoughts,
it is only due to them believing that too!!!!

When you love yourself and others,
no lower thought can harm you...

But a harmful thought will harm the person who thought it,
Because they are on the level of receiving those lower thoughts.

Rise up to the levels of love, joy, peace and comfort,
to receive more of those higher level of thought.

Peace be with you too

My dear, you want to win happiness and love!!

........and then you lose depression.
Exchange one for the other ok.

Focus on all the things that make you happy and that you love....
You will feel better soon.

Peace be with you child
.
.
.
You are clinging to a belief that is now harmful to you, and arguing with others about it is proof that you are not at peace with yourself at this time.

Humans have the same chemicals since the dark ages, and just because someone has decided that there is an imbalance does not create a cure, it creates more stress.

Please understand that to balance your chemicals, as you believe, is to know that in this moment Now, everything is ok...

Is it?
Do you have everything you need in this moment Now?
Do you?

That is what this post is trying to get you to understand.

Take no notice of others who are pushing your anger buttons my dear, they find it funny winding you up.

They are only words ok.

Other than that, is everything else OK at this very moment Now?
This is the recipe to create your good life.
Although, it may be too difficult to let your label,
of who you believe are now, to go.

Sometimes you get more attention by being sick.
That's ok too.
When you are ready to feel better you now know what to do.
.

Your judgement of her keeps that aspect of her with you.

See her differently by acting differently with her.
Ask her out for a cup of tea to discuss something...

Everything is ok.

Peace be with you

.

.

.
Smile
Smile
Smile
Smile
Smile
Smile
Smile
Smile
Smile
Getting the hang of it yet?
Smile
Smile
Smile
Smile
Smile
Smile
Now you will feel better sooner.

Smile
Know everything is ok
Smile.
Smile.
Smile.
Smile.
Smile
Smile
Smile
Smile
Smile

.

.

OK....
Perfection recognises no imperfection.

So, to remember you are perfect,
is to remove all imperfection by its lack of attention.

You are so focused on the imperfection that you create more and suffer its effects.

Focus on every cell that is perfect.
Create more perfection
Feel more perfection
See more perfection
Because
You are perfection....

You just have been around too many people who only see and speak of your imperfection....
And that is not real.

Perfection is reality.
Peace be with you and your family
.
.
.
Smile....
That is your protection my dear!

No lower energy can penetrate anyone who feels good in their smile.

Peace be with you child
.
.
.
.
Smile....
It is not your business what others think about you.

It is your business to be the best you can be,
in being a kind person,
and love unconditionally, those sent for you to be kind to.

Peace be with you
.

Love yourself more....
Look in the mirror and forgive yourself for the past,
And know that it is all gone.
All the bad stuff....is gone.
It is gone.

Now look at yourself and see your lovely self and know you are worthy of all the good that is given to you in word and action.
You are worth it,
and only you can choose to feel this worth and this love of your self.

Self love enables confidence....
confide nce = confide with yourself.

Have a good chat and tell yourself about all the good that you are.....
And that confidence is then felt by others who also feel confident in all you can achieve.

Peace be with you

.
.
.
.

Love cures all internal problems
And 'prevents' all internal problems.

The heart is the seat of one's love, and when the heart breaks, other parts within the body break down as well.

To return to thoughts of love will repair any damage,
with feeling and happiness.

Turn your family's mind to all that they love and remember all that they loved.
Talk about what people love.
Get them to feel love again.

Keep this feeling going and life's experiences will get so much better very quickly.

Peace be with you and your family

.
.

Actually, they do love you...
You just block their love by your feelings of
not being worthy of love.
Or not actually wanting their love.

That is ok too.

Love is with you now...

Sit, be still, smile and feel that love now.
Feel it deep within you.
Smile deep in your tummy and feel good in that smile.

To feel good and know how that feels,
will help you through the day,
meeting other people,
and feeling that love for them.

Phew, that feels better.

Peace be with you and your family
.
.
.
.
(Never) forget them!
Forgive and give thanks for their lessons in life that they have taught you.

If you don't know what they are...
It is always about how much you love and love unconditionally.
.
.
.
Love us not unkindness is it...!

So perhaps that is where you are needing clarity.

Love us a high energy.
Unkindness is low energy,
Yet it is still energy.

Is that more understandable?.
Peace be with you

Love my dear,

What made you fall in love with this man?

Go back to that memory and really feel that love again...
Speak words of kindness and gentleness in your thoughts and conversations.

You will then create enough vibrational force to create a loving environment in which you all live.

He will change when you do my dear.
It is your thoughts and judgement that have created this lower experience and suffering.

Peace be with you and your family now.

.

.

.

.

R ealizing
I
C reate
H appiness

So, it is necessary to be RICH...

Peace be with you child

.

.

.

.

As soon as you have more faith in yourself,
More people will be interested in all you have to offer.

To believe in their resistance to your craft, creates all that you believe in.

Reiki needs a pure belief to enable its perfect result.
So practice on your own resistance, and then just see what happens without you even asking.

Peace be with you

Smile
Congratulations
Your words create....

Your words... Yours!!!

My words create for me!
Your words create for me if I believe you,
but I stopped believing in harmful words, so I have a better life.

My words create in you, if you believe them.

You are the keeper of your own mind.

Be thankful you know this now.
Now you can start creating your new life experience by using good and kind words about yourself and others.

You will notice a change as quickly as you are prepared to accept it.

Anyone who speaks or writes harmful and bad words can only harm themselves,
when you believe only in goodness and kindness.

That is your so called 'protection' my dears.

Your own goodness protects you from all words that are harmful.
Your own badness and hurtful words only harm yourself.

So you might want to read your texts and posts back to yourself to see which ones you delete.
If it feels bad when you read your words, that you wrote,
then delete them, for they only harm you.

You are all worthy of this knowledge.

You are all perfect, apart from your hurtful words to each other.

Choose your words to create a good life experience.
You are worthy of your Love.

What do you believe in?

Past life death experience?

Or
Stop watching those sort of movies
that keep playing when you sleep and you become a member of the cast.....
Until you become the Director!

Enjoy your life now.
Be careful what you watch and read.

Peace be with you

.
.

.
Smile and
What are you thankful for?

Really?
What are you thankful for?

To be in gratitude for all the good in your life
will raise your spirits up and keep you happy...

Yes, it's called counting your blessings

You know as soon as you feel bad again,
That you have changed your mind from gratitude, kindness and love...
To poor ole me!

Poor ole me stays poor in good mental health.

Be RICH in good health by knowing.....

R emembering
I
C reate
H appiness

Peace be with you

Smile....

Keep smiling.
And then open the door,
and walk away.

Come back again when you are in sufficient strength.
.
.
.
You are made of energy.

You are either connected to the source of good thoughts that produce more high energy in you....

Or you are in a lower negative state that is a low energy.

Your mind controls the flow....
By the thoughts it accepts.

You accept good thoughts or one's that don't make you feel good
.... and so you think you are having energy sucked from you...

So you can blame someone else...!!!!

It is always your choice....
To love.
To not judge.
To be kind.

Then you feel fantastic.

Peace be with you too
.
.
.
You let it in.
Now let it go.
You chose it.
You can release it.
You accepted it.
You free it.
You Love it.
.

Congratulations
Now you know fear.

Do everything you can to be it's opposite.
And that is always Love.

Love them all.
Love your situation.
Love your kids.
Be kind to yourself,
and everyone else.

Then you won't be in fear.

You won't have anything to complain about either,
and that can be difficult to get used to...
But it's worth it.

It is always your choice to think a kind thought, or a horrid thought.

You are experiencing your past horrid thoughts.
Create a better future now.
Change your mind now.

Peace be with you and your family
.
.
.
Best never be brutal ok...

So now you know how powerful your thoughts are....

Forgive yourself.
Laugh at your silliness.

And love your hearing again.
Know that it is there and sit and listen to the sounds again.
Don't force anything,
just know you can hear.

You just let it go for a while.

Well done.
Be more careful ok.

Accept it as if you had chosen it....

Phew, that feels better.

Peace be with you child

.
.

Smile and Congratulations,
You needed to rest!
Your body knows when it's time to rest.
So it gets you to rest in the only way it knows how,
by shutting down.

So, relax.
Enjoy the rest.
When you accept it as if you had planned it,
rest is much easier.
You get well sooner.

And a child is always influenced by its parents.
... That's why they call it influenza...!

Rest easy. Enjoy your rest.
What better time to rest together and enjoy each other.
Peace be with you and your family.
.
.

Actually, judgement and low feeling thoughts drain your energy...

Love never drains you.
So love them anyway...
And love yourself too.

You will soon feel full of energy again....
Then walk away, smiling.

Peace be with you too

Smile
By saying....

'I am strong'

Peace be with you
.
.
.
When you practice good thoughts,

it's a bit like going to the gym,
it's only as good as when you put the effort in.

When you know you actually have a choice
to accept only the good thoughts,
that create the good words,
that create the higher emotions...
Then it gets easier.

Sadness is due to the build up of low thoughts.
Just like a dripping tap filling a cup.
Bad thought after another will keep you low and full of them.

So when you know that,
it is your choice to think good thoughts,
to be kind to each other and yourself...
Then you start to rise up in your emotions.

It's all easy when you understand the Laws of Mentality,
Polarity and Cause and Effect....

We are sad because we haven't learnt the proper way to be happy...
We have to work out with Good thoughts,
Good words and Goodness....

Or you remain in the lower emotions and suffer...

Now you know
You have a choice...
So it is easy....

It's not easy when you don't want to work at being happy.
Peace be with you

You have no control over another person.

You can only love and guide them with kindness,
and one day,
they remember that kindness,
and return to receive more of what they need.

Teach kindness and love, and that is what they give to others...
And to you!

Peace be with you and your family

You think you cannot hear...?
So you cannot hear.

What was happening at the time of your hearing loss?
What didn't you want to hear..!?

Please sit with that question for a while....
Remember....

What didn't you want to hear?

Forgive that time...
Forgive
And
Smile at the thoughts that stopped you hearing.

You are perfect,
accept that sweetheart.

The past has gone.
Forgive yourself and those involved.

Today is a brand new day full of lovely sounds to hear
And some horrid ones too...
Just stick your fingers in your ears and walk away.

You are perfect and everything is functioning correctly.

Just keep loving them.

Send them loving thoughts.

Feel good when you think about them.

Sound happy and loving when they call.

Peace be with you
.
.
.
.

That choice was made due to thoughts from the past that had created the Now.

Now you feel the compassion.

Now, use what you feel you need to do next.
Now.
And what do you feel you need to do Now?

And Now do you feel different?
And Now are your thoughts different and so you want to do something else?

And Now....

Are you getting the hang of this yet?

Smile Now.
Now go love him again.

Now stay and think some more.

Now say you are sorry.
Now don't.

Now live in peace.
Now don't.

It is all your choice Now!

Anxiety comes from not knowing what the future holds for you and Anxiety creates more internal breakdown of organs.

So that is why the POWER OF NOW is to be fully understood.......
NOW.....now......now in this moment now!

...without any thought of what has been said to you in the past, which makes you look forward with dread.

Who would you be without that conversation that has been put into your mind?
You would be perfect...
because you are..!

And as you accept your perfection,
you create more of it.
And as you create and believe more in perfection,
Now you become more perfect.

The more you believe in what others say as hurtful,
the more you create that.

TAKE BACK YOUR POWER and stay in the NOW,
this moment now where you are on the new path to perfection.

Because we have just programmed you with a new thought form of perfection that you can believe in.......
If you want to.

Just as it is your choice to believe in what hurt others program you with.

Your non-perfection has been built up over time with thoughts of fear that it could happen to you
....thus, it has.......

NOW, YOUR POWER IS IN KNOWING THAT YOU CAN NOW BELIEVE IN PERFECTION....
AND EVERY DAY IN EVERY WAY, YOU BECOME MORE PERFECT...BECAUSE THAT IS WHAT YOU BELIEVE IN.....

How can we prove to you that this is true....?

Because you have believed in the other experience, and well done, you created that too!

So, SIT, BE STILL AND FOCUS ON WHAT YOU WANT NOW.

Perfect this
and
Perfect that,

SMILE at your silliness of forgetting this Truth.
Now you have been reminded.

It is up to you to turn this ship around and head for port Perfection.

Well done Captain for wanting to know the Truth at last.

Peace is now with you....
should you wish to accept that too!

.
.
.
.
.
.

The cost is whatever you feel you need to pay...
And a good mentor will inform you that you pay until you no longer feel you need to pay...

So perhaps you will know that sooner now!

Ask someone to help you.
Offer to pay them and see what they say.

It is always between you and them.

Peace be with you child

.
.
.
.

You experience trauma,
so you know you can get through it....!
Life is easier then.

.

When you feel low...
you have to Smile.

A good feel good Smile deep in your tummy,
and that will raise you to a higher level of good thoughts.
And the more good thoughts you have....
the more good thoughts you keep on experiencing.

You get to choose the thought you wish to experience.

Do you feel good or bad?
You then in that instant keep feeling good with another good thought or Smile,
and choose a better feeling thought.

....or experience the bad feeling,
and just know that it is a comparison thought.
It is an opposite,
that is all.
And it is easier to relieve yourself of it,
as you are remaining calm and accepting the next thought,
and choosing how you want to feel.

Peace be with you
.
.
.
.
.
NOW feels fantastic doesn't it.
.
.
.
.
.
You needed to learn more,
and so you took longer than him.
And you are always learning more.
It is a great journey,
enjoy it.
.
.
.
.

Its a practice....
like going to the gym and pumping up your muscles.
You pump your mind in good thoughts and kindness, to self and others.
It then becomes easier and you stay on track.

.
.
.

Sit, be still....
Smile and feel that smile deep within your tummy.
Feel that smile go into your tummy and feel good in that smile.
Feel good, take the time to feel good within yourself,
to heal the wounds the mind is causing by negative thought.

Focus on the inner body and not the mind.
Accept that everything will turn out for the best,
and you can feel good about this moment now,
and that will create a better future for you and your children.

And you can teach them this process,
so they too remain calm and heal themselves,
with the Peace and Love of Jesus Christ within them in that Smile.
Love feels good.....
Feel good and get better sooner in Peace.

.
.
.

I use Jesus Christ alot. Yes I do...
...because I just write words.

I write words.
I use words that feel good and make me feel good.
The story of Jesus Christ is there for you to learn more love and
kindness, so I use His name so you remember His kindness to others.

I try to forget the horrid stuff, and know that we too can harm ourselves
when we start to believe in all that we read....just as He did.

Be careful what you read, watch, listen to and believe.
Take your time and feel good in all that you believe.

Be kind to yourself.
Peace be with you.

.
.

Know that you are always looked after,
when you ask for the guidance of Jesus Christ.
You will know what to do for the best when you remain calm.

I had to re-boot and allow all the new info to sink in,
and feel good about it.
I kept popping back and found it was still good,
and that I had to create my own goodness,
to be balanced with the new info.
Thank you for asking.

Focus on what you want....
and the other stuff moves out of your experience.

Sit...
be still and love them.
You loved them yesterday.
Love them again today.
Only Love takes away the pain,
for there is no pain when you love.
Forgive and Love.
You will soon feel better again..

When we are hurt,
we hurt the ones we love.

We forget we only hurt the ones we love.
And so we forgive ourselves and love them anyway.

Smile, sweetheart,
Love doesn't hurt.
Love kept you together.

Lack of Love and your judgements hurt.
Forgive yourself for not knowing how to stay in Love.

Love doesn't hurt,
because as soon as you Love,
the hurt goes away.

Think kind thoughts.
Speak kind words.
Love will soon return and make you feel better again.

Thank you for asking for this book.

Thank you for buying this book.

You are welcome to ask me a question on Facebook page....
'Sally Ann Slight'.

I look forward to helping you too.

Peace be with you....always.

Yogi Sally Ann Slight
Dartmouth
Devon
UK

Yoga Life Coach & Good Health Motivator.
Yoga Siromani taught at Sivananda Ashram, Bahamas 2007.
Masseuse/Motivator to EDDIE KIDD (after his accident),
and the SUPER BIKERS at BRANDS HATCH Race Circuit, Kent,
Life Coach/Motivator to Servicemen with addictions & P.T.S.D.

Just as Yoga Asana classes keep your body flexible and healthy, you also need a flexible mind to regain strength and happiness to improve your life situation.

To understand your emotions and feelings, and how to change them, will bring you great success in reaching any of your life ambitions or embarking upon a change in career...or enabling you to cope with loss or suffering from depression.

Health has a root, and the root is based within the mind, and when you are understanding your emotions you can then weed out sickness and negative paths and return your life of happiness.

You have the CHOICE to be happy or sad!...it is a good habit that will give you the understanding to regain, and maintain, your health, happiness and success again.

27th January 2020 ...2nd edition

www.ingramcontent.com/pod-product-compliance
Lightning Source LLC
Chambersburg PA
CBHW031451070426
42452CB00038B/793